A JIHAD
FOR LOVE

MOHAMED EL BACHIRI is a former
metro driver from Brussels. His wife
Loubna was killed in the Brussels
bombing of March 2016, leaving behind
three young children. *A Jihad for Love*
topped the Dutch bestseller list a week
after publication in March 2017.

A JIHAD
FOR LOVE

Mohamed El Bachiri

with DAVID VAN REYBROUCK

Translated from the Dutch by Sam Garrett

HEAD
of ZEUS

First published in Dutch by De Bezige Bij, Amsterdam, 2017

This English translation first published in the UK in 2017
by Head of Zeus, Ltd.

9 7 5 3 1 2 4 6 8

A catalogue record for this book is available from
the British Library.

ISBN (PB): 9781786698001
ISBN (E): 9781786697998

Printed and bound in Great Britain by
CPI Group (UK) Ltd, Croydon CR0 4YY

Head of Zeus Ltd
First Floor East
5–8 Hardwick Street
London EC1R 4RG
WWW.HEADOFZEUS.COM

Jihad (adj., m)

(Arab.: *jihād*, effort, struggle on God's way
    1. Effort every Muslim must make to combat
       his own passions. (Referred to by the
       prophet Mohammed as the 'greater jihad')
    2. Struggle to defend the domain of Islam.
       (Referred to as the 'lesser jihad'.)

Larousse, Dictionnaire de français.

Loubna, my dearest,
Nothing has flavour any more, nothing has
purpose any more.
My dreams were yours, your dreams were mine.
Growing old together, hand in hand.
Watching the children grow up, in joy and love.
That was our path, drawn out by the One who
holds the pen of fate.

At least that's what we thought.

But, to our great sorrow, a different fate was
waiting for us.

You were my mate, my confidante, my best
friend.
Love of my life, mother of my children, the one
with whom I always laughed.
Our relationship was serious, but we never took
ourselves too seriously.

Our story was built on love, trust and respect.
Simple, but powerful love.

What an extremely rare pearl I had.
She brought me so much joy, simply by being
beside me.
What luck to have such a beautiful, intelligent
wife with such a big heart…
We always protected our children against war
and madness.
But the worst of it, alas, has come over us.

Face to face with what no one can comprehend,
what am I supposed to tell the children?

That day

I had the day off.
She took the metro.
One of her girlfriends rang the bell.
She said there had been an attack.
Right away, I had a bad feeling about it.
I saw that the 9:10 had never gone online.
Then I knew all I needed to know.
I went to my parents'.
Wrapped in a blanket, I collapsed.

For the rest, I have a sort of amnesia.
I'm in a different dimension.
That is the only way I can go on living.

The evening

Once they're all in bed, I write sometimes, on the
screen of my telephone. Texts and sentences that
flash through my mind, poems sometimes.
Writing, finding words, true words.

By writing about love, I come closer to your
shining face.

The night

It's the middle of the night.
I go down the stairs.
Everything is spinning.
Where am I?
The littlest is awake.
He's crying.
He's hungry.
He is three years old.
Our youngest.
We have three.
Three sons. Ten, eight and three years old.
Our children.
'My children,' I should say now.

Her name is still beside the doorbell.
Of course. This is her house.
Even if she doesn't live here any more.
Even if she's doesn't live at all any more.

She was a light sleeper, I slept soundly.
When we were first married, I had to get used
to that.
There was so much to get used to.
The regular routine, the living together, all
those things.
I liked to fall asleep reading a book.
I had to learn that light can bother others.
I had to learn to think more of others.

Now I don't sleep any more.
Without pills, I can't.
I barely eat.
I've lost pounds, don't ask me how many.
I wore medium, now I'm a small.
I had to give away a whole pile of clothes.

The boy is awake.
He's crying.
Everything spins.
It's because of the pills.
I fall.
I go down the stairs.
I make his bottle.
I fall again.

I fall.
This is how I live now.
This is where I'm standing now.

My voice

I don't know if I'm going to come back to life,
real, living life.
I'm here for my children.
Just consider me a dead man.
A dead man giving a lesson in life.

My parents

Do I really have to talk about my own life?
Anecdotes are unimportant; I already know
them all.
Details no longer count: this is not a biography.
But there are a few elements that might help to
throw open the windows of my message.

I am a product of the first wave of immigrants.
My father knew poverty. He was born in 1940, not
far from Nador, in northern Morocco. The Rif.
His family moved to Oran, in French Algeria, like
so many Moroccan families did back then. After
that he left for France, then to Germany. In 1963
he arrived in Brussels, with a friend who would
later become his brother-in-law.

My mother's family had moved to French Algeria
too, to find work. That's where my mother was

born, in 1951. After Algeria became independent in 1962, the family went back to Morocco and settled in Oujda, close to the Algerian border.

My parents got married in Morocco and my eldest sister was born there too. Like the rest of my brothers and sisters, I was born in Belgium, in Sint-Agatha-Berchem, not far from Molenbeek. That was in 1980. I'm the sixth of eight children: five girls and three boys. We've always lived in Molenbeek. Our house was on Bevrijdersplein, close to Jubelfeestlaan.

My father worked as a tram driver in Brussels, later he got a job in a factory. Then he became a shopkeeper, he had a grocery shop in Schaarbeek and in Molenbeek. Because he'd experienced so much hardship while he was growing up, he always stressed how lucky we were to be living in Belgium, a country where we had the means to grow. Getting an education gave us new opportunities. We needed to be grateful to this country and, at the same time, hold on to our own culture.

Language

My father spoke French with us. That wasn't
the obvious thing for him to do, because his
native language was Tamazight, what they also
call 'Berber'.
But he insisted that we speak French, so that we
would have a thorough command of the language.
He had learned French while he was in Algeria.
Later on, he taught himself Arabic, from books.
He learned the Arabic alphabet in order to read
the Koran.

My parents spoke Tamazight with each other.
That was useful when they wanted to talk about
something the children weren't supposed to hear.
But now that's a handicap for us. I can follow a
conversation in Tamazight, I understand it a bit,
but when I open my mouth and try to speak it,
I sound ridiculous. My Arabic is limited too.

When I go to Morocco, that complicates things. My accent is that of Oujda, so people tend to think I'm Algerian.

French is really my native language. I always speak French, with my brothers and sisters, at school and at home. Of course, our French has some Arabic words in it. In Brussels we say *drari* for boy and *sahbe* for friend. When someone lets himself be fooled, he's *h'ché*, and when he's done something stupid he's *hayak*. And when someone doubts what we say, we say *wallah*, I swear.
By God!

Faith

I'm a Muslim, first of all by birth, then by conviction.

I inherited Islam. The faith played a major role in our family. My parents stressed its moral values: uprightness, friendliness, a sense of honour and keeping one's word. At home, we prayed five times a day. Our father introduced us to it at an early age, but everyone did with it what they wanted.

We took Arabic lessons, in other to learn the language and be able to recite the Koran. That went in the old-fashioned way: boys and girls in separate classrooms, at a local mosque close to our house. We had to learn the Koran by rote – not by heart. In fact, we recited it without understanding it. In the 1980s, anyone who felt like it could call himself a teacher. Ours was old and strict. He slapped our fingers with a ruler. He hit me too, a few times. The worst thing was when my friends would organise a football tournament and I had to go to Arabic lessons. So that Arabic school didn't last too long. I still know a few *suras*, maybe thirteen or fourteen of them, only the ones essential for saying my prayers.

The Koran is poetry, in Arabic it's a beautiful text. The Arabs used the Word and the poetry to make contact, to discuss, to convince. It was beauty. It was art. In this religion, poetry plays a crucial role. How someone who was first a shepherd, later a merchant and then finally a mystic discovered poetry as his driving force…. You may criticise the Koran, but as poetry it is without equal.

My school

I went to a Catholic primary school, because it was close by. Saint-Joseph Saint-Rémy. That went fairly well. In the late 1980s, a lot of children from the Moroccan community went there. Of course, we got lessons in the Catholic faith and learned about Catholic values. But my father said: 'It's just like with us, except Jesus is not the son of God and we have an extra prophet.'

Voilà, it was as simple as that.

Christmas was a lovely time, that atmosphere of brotherhood, peace and love. I was always a little jealous of the other children. At home we didn't have a Christmas tree and no presents either. But we watched the Christmas stories on TV together. Wonderful films for the whole family. It was magical.

I've never considered becoming a Catholic. but I already felt a bond with them. We see Christ as an earlier prophet, so we already had a bit of Christianity in us. I felt it would be a loss to turn my back on Islam. We were taught that the Koran was the word of God, while the Bible, the New Testament, was just a story.

Compassion

As a Muslim, I was lucky enough to share some lovely moments and to receive a lot of loving care from the teaching staff at my Catholic school. As an adult, I feel only the deepest fondness, admiration and friendship for the Catholic community. Those expressions of love and charity are not something one quickly forgets.

So I encourage Muslims to show the same kind of charitable spirit towards followers of other faiths: Christians, Jews, Buddhists, atheists and agnostics. That is the best possible answer to those who want to sow dissension among us, the Muslims of the West. I oppose religious fundamentalism – no matter whether it comes from Muslims or from people of other religions.

Would God really blame us for showing love

towards people who think differently from us?
After all, He is the creator of all peoples and
nations. As the Koran puts it so beautifully:
'O mankind! We created you from a single male
and female, and made you into nations and tribes,
that ye may know each other.'*

* The Koran, Al-Hujraat, 49:13

The Koran

In the Koran one finds a timeless, vertical
storyline that has to do with our relationship with
the Supreme Being, with God.
And then you have passages with a horizontal
orientation, the ones that deal with rules. When
it comes to those passages, it is important to be
reasonable and to look at the context: the texts,
after all, date back to the seventh century.

Islam assumes that the people it is talking to are
reasonable people. Some texts even say: 'And
those are the ones endued with understanding.'*
That, after all, is what distinguishes us from the
animals, as Aristotle said long ago. We have been
given reason so that we can think, and thinking is
a divine gift. The problem is that it is possible to
know a lot without being reasonable. The point is

* The Koran, Az-Zumar, 39:18

25

to be able to put those two things together!
On the one hand one has the Prophet while he
was still in Mecca, on the other is the Prophet
who has gone to Medina. The Prophet in
Mecca is a mystic whose message doesn't differ
much from Christ's: focus on God. But in Medina,
where he had fled, he was asked to mediate
between the different religious communities.
Because of his reputation for being just, he
became a leader, whether he liked it or not.

Imagine that Christ, with his beautiful message,
had suddenly become a tribal or national leader.
Would his message have remained the same?
Wouldn't his vision have changed? When you
are forced to practise politics, everything
suddenly becomes so much more concrete,
so much more worldly.

The Prophet operated in a specific historical
context, in a world where slavery was still
common and where having a daughter almost
amounted to a curse. Still, he called for the
emancipation of slaves and women. To the
moment of his death, he remained a humanist

and a feminist. He was a Prophet who remained very much open to others, who entered into a dialogue with his age.

For us, as Muslims with common sense, it is obvious and necessary to see the belligerent passages in the Koran as historical words from the seventh century. It would be an absolute mistake to try to claim that they are universally valid. And they may never, ever be used to harm another person.

Let's act with our reason and with our hearts! There is nothing spiritual or transcendent about murder or war: they have to do with relationships between people, with territories you want to defend or expand. Is a military victory a victory for God? Are the cries of the dying a symphony to the greater glory of God? What's religious about one people exterminating another people?

Reflection

So Muslims would go to Paradise, but not the rest of the world? And unbelievers, like my teachers at school, so they were doomed too? I couldn't figure that. I still can't figure that.

At primary school we learned about Mother Teresa. So that woman, who gave her life to others, who set aside her own life in order to perform good work, so she was going to Hell too? I asked my father about it. He said: 'People like her will not suffer in their graves. But they're not Muslims, so they won't go to Paradise.' That seemed unfair to me. Why not her, while a common, everyday person who never did anything for anyone else would find the gates of Paradise opened wide for them, simply because they're a Muslim?

My father's answer puzzled me, but I didn't want to play the Che Guevara of the family. My father stuck to the sermons of our imam, and I can understand that. His primary task was to raise his children well and to establish a connection between our religion and the values of this country, not necessarily to carry out endless philosophical and theological discussions.

But even in my circles, when one questions something, the answer is often enough: 'You don't have enough knowledge and insight to give your opinion.' I don't agree with that. Each one of us has the capacity to reflect, we have been given intelligence in order that we can ask relevant questions. Some people have lots of knowledge to fall back on, but still have a closed mind. But tell me, isn't an open mind more important that pure knowledge?

The ability to think is a gift from God. You need to cherish that, you may use that. So many people have developed insights that have helped mankind to advance; that is a divine wonder. To just shove that all aside because it doesn't happen to be

Islamic shows a true lack of respect for the rest
of humanity, and forces you to ignore all kinds of
valuable things.

Curiosity

As far as I'm concerned, wisdom begins with curiosity.

I've always been curious about the history of the West and the East. I've always had a desire to learn and to meet other people. At school I was a rather playful pupil; I was full of humour and hijinks. I liked to joke around when we were supposed to be working, when we were supposed to be serious, and so I had to stay after sometimes. But I was wild about the classes in world-orientation; they were about the universe, about history, about the Celts of ancient Gaul. I read comic books based on Greek mythology, I was a fan of Asterix.

When you succeed in stimulating a young child's curiosity, you're in fact inviting that person to find out about others.

I truly love history. Ancient history, the Middle Ages, the Renaissance, the colonial era. And by that I mean history without biases: a son is in no way responsible for his father's mistakes. But history has to be known and acknowledged, so that we can all make progress together.

The future? It starts with history.

History

Generally speaking, Muslims don't know much about the history of Islam. But human thought evolves. Islam is a religion about which people have done a lot of thinking and, obviously, about which a lot more thinking will take place. By learning the history of Islam, you find out that there have been all sorts of views, all different varieties of openness. Tenth-century Baghdad was an amazing place. Scholars there analysed the thinking of the Greeks, the Indians, the Persians…

Islam is not one thing. It has many faces.

These days, many Muslims are afraid of getting lost. 'Don't ask so many questions! It will only confuse you!' That shows how unsure people can be about their faith. Some of them measure the credibility of an imam by the length of his beard.

Please, abundant growth on the chin isn't a sign of wisdom, is it? When you're sure of yourself, you can go very far and still always find your way back.

I have a lot of respect for Martin Luther: you have to be awfully sure of yourself to turn against the Church like that! Risking his own neck, he still did it, because he was god-fearing and devoted. When he saw the contrast between the 'poor entering the Kingdom of Heaven' and the riches of the Vatican, when he understood all that business about paying indulgences... he asked himself a couple of highly relevant questions.

The history of religion in Europe is filled with violence. The Inquisition, the Reformation, wars...

Self-confidence

It seems to me that there's a lack of self-confidence in my surroundings. Among my friends there is a fear of being wrong, of making errors in reasoning, of seeing things incorrectly.

I've had that same feeling myself. As a child, I sincerely believed that blonde girls were better than brunettes; I clearly had a complex about the colour of my skin. Added to that, our parents were constantly emphasizing that we owed a debt of gratitude to Belgium. There was always a sort of sense of obligation towards this country that had welcomed us – even though we had never asked to be born here, or anywhere else for that matter!

I was six the first time someone called me a 'dirty Moroccan'. It was a neighbour of ours, a man of Greek origin, who shouted it from a balcony across the street. It was meant as a joke, but it hurt me. I went inside and closed the doors to the balcony. Since then, I've been called that a few times. But the good thing about Molenbeek was that we were all in it together. The residents of Belgian origin had all bailed out, there weren't a lot of them left. We had Flemish neighbours who never spoke to us. My father said they were racists; he had tried to strike up a conversation with them. I think they were in a state of shock, after that sudden wave of immigrants. And I can understand that. Change is always frightening.

I didn't know what to say back to that 'dirty Moroccan'. At school they didn't teach us that Belgium needed immigrants. If they had, I could have said: 'Hey, listen, it's your country that asked my father to come and work here!' So instead of self-confidence, I felt more like I was on a lower level, that I owed something to others.

And during adolescence, of course, you start doubting everything. Why should you feel grateful to a country where you happened to be born, just like everyone else, but where other people still

called you a 'dirty Moroccan', even though that
same country invited your father's generation to
come and work there?

Travel

In secondary school, I was a miserable student.
Mathematics made me sick. I had a real phobia
when it came to numbers. I went to public secondary school; that, of course, is what our hardworking,
proletarian fathers really wanted. Their dream was
that we would go to college and become lawyers or
doctors. But the teachers didn't pass that passion
along to us, that hunger for learning. I flunked my
third year and then my fifth, and at the age of eight-
een I dropped out of school without a diploma. My
parents weren't happy about that, but I did it grad-
ually. I told my father that I was going to explore
other possibilities, but in fact I went right from the
classroom to my first job. I went to work as a temp
at the airport, doing night shifts and sorting mail for
the TNT. That allowed me to travel, just by looking
at all that mail. There were destinations all over the
world, written on the front of those envelopes.

Meeting

One day she came into the shop.

By that time, I had a job selling mobile phones
in Anderlecht. She came in to buy a phone.
I remember that first time we met, her eyes.
There was no play of seduction involved.
I was simply interested and curious.
I wanted to get to know her, she seemed very
pretty and very intelligent. Not a made-up kind
of beauty, no, a natural beauty, a person with
nothing artificial about them.
Neither inside nor out.

I was twenty-three.

She had a beautiful face, big eyes, a lovely nose, a
sweet mouth that was made even prettier by her
beautiful smile that ended in dimples at both ends.

Her face radiated so much love, so much goodness.

Loubna…

Relationship

I gave her my number, without giving myself
much of a chance, really. But a few days later, she
called. That first time we went to drink something
at the old covered market, the Sint-Gorikshallen.
The weather was warm.

She had just completed teaching college, to
become a physical education instructor. She was
nine months younger than me. In the period
that followed, I saw her regularly. She was an
intelligent girl with a very open mind, which was
a good match for my own way of looking at life.
My family came from the Rif, in the north,
where people are generally more withdrawn.
She was from Salé, close to Rabat, where people
tend to be more open. But it clicked between us,
right from the start. She was a Muslim too,
but she didn't wear a headscarf, she didn't feel

that was necessary for the path she meant to follow in life.

She lived in Schaarbeek. Six months later we became engaged. We announced it officially to the family. My parents went to her parents and asked for her hand. It was hard for my mother to accept my leaving home.

On 20 November 2004, we had the civil ceremony, a few weeks later we threw a party and invited everyone. After the civil wedding and after receiving the imam's blessing, we moved into an apartment in Schaarbeek. It wasn't far from where she worked, at the Islamic Al-Ghazi School. There weren't a lot of female gym teachers.

Living together

Living together went well, but we had to get used to it. I loved to cook, but I always dirtied about twenty pans. The food was good, but the kitchen looked as though a hurricane had hit. I was so much sloppier than she was. I'm a sort of Diogenes. She was very organised. I had to learn to temper myself a bit.

We also had to learn how to communicate. When I read that book, *Men are from Mars, Women are from Venus*, it came as a revelation to me. We men sometimes get things all wrong, we don't always understand what women mean. When a man gets lost in a strange city, for example, he'll make a decision and follow the traffic signs. But then the woman says he needs to turn here or there, so the man thinks: What is this? Does she think I can't find my way? He sees it as an attack on his masculinity. Even though the woman's only thinking: I love him, I'm going to help him.

You have couples where the man is constantly trying to prove to the woman what he's capable of, but he forgets what it's really all about. Sometimes a woman doesn't need anything but a shoulder, a willing ear or attention, and not someone who tries to give her the world on a platter.

I'm all for equal dealings between men and women, that's enormously enriching. But there's no denying those differences in sensitivities and experience. You have to keep working constantly on understanding each other, on getting to know each other better.

Love is something you have to work at, absolutely. And you have to cherish her, just like you do your faith.

In the first few months we had arguments about senseless things. Later we stopped arguing almost altogether. Loubna and I dealt with each other very peacefully. We fit well together, we were totally in contact. We shared the same ideas about the world, about things and about Islam. We shared the same love for others.

Loubna, in fact, is speaking through everything I say here.

What's more, we supported each other in our plans. We called each other at work every day, to ask how it was going. I had found a job as a metro rail driver. I worked from afternoon till evening in that dark, underground Brussels, but whenever we had a break we called each other. We were like a couple of overgrown children. We were always pulling jokes on each other. One time, I replaced one of her girlfriend's numbers with mine, in the contact list of her mobile phone, and when she called I imitated her friend's voice. Sometimes I would start talking like an elderly Moroccan, or do an African accent. Man, we laughed so much during those twelve years.

Marriage

The way she looked at me: she made me more handsome, richer, bigger. I blossomed forth completely. I felt like the luckiest man on earth. It is such a joy to keep the company of a pleasant person. I was very proud of who she was, but I didn't go around showing her off. She was my friend, not my trophy. She was my best friend, my mate. That relationship gave me complete fulfilment. Within Islam, they say that a marriage is the half of all faith. I always added: 'And the divorce is the other half.' Only kidding.
In the Koran, God talks about the blessings of marriage.

For me, that was:

I love, therefore I live.
I love, therefore I am.

Birth

I was there when the children were born.
Those were the loveliest moments of my life.
Now it hurts so badly to think about it.

About the attacks

He leaves me cold, that guy.

Goodness

How can I write about love without talking
about Loubna?
That unique person with her unparalleled beauty
and her endless goodness.
A dream in broad daylight, united with my other
half, in my heart forever.
A symbol of love, beauty and eternal youth.
The best wife you could imagine for the husband
I was.
Her wonder at the beautiful things in the world.
Her loathing for violence and war.
Her independence, her enthusiasm, her generosity.
That lovely, soft Loubna embodied the good and
the beautiful in the world.
How can I describe love without singing that
woman's praises?
That committed woman who helped women to
move because sports can be a force for freedom.

That dedicated woman, the courageous mother,
full of love for her three children.
That queen of hearts who never missed a charity
gathering.
The woman who won the hearts of all those who
crossed her path.
What a loss!

Thanks to God's grace, your man will come to you
across the firmament, for an embrace and a dance
beneath the shower of stars that will once again
light up your angel's face.

The children

I told the children that Mama was in heaven,
that bad people had planted a bomb in the metro,
that God had wanted to protect her and that was
why he'd picked her up and taken her with him
to heaven.

To them, life is just stupid. A mother who says
goodbye, gives them a kiss and goes to work, and
after that no more Mama. They don't get it. They
saw Mama in the paper.

Brotherhood

'We are all brothers,' I say.
'Is a person who does something like that also
a brother?'
'Yes, he is also a brother, but a brother who's taken
a wrong turn. As a human being, he remains your
brother, even if he's done the worst thing.'

They are furious, they want revenge. I tell them:
'If you kill someone or answer violence with
violence, you make the same mistake they did.
You lower yourself to their level. You boys are
better than that.'

Vengeance

I am the only captain left on a ship with three
crew members, on an ocean of sorrow.
The wind blows hard, speaking your sweet name,
blowing us towards the unknown.
Without you I have lost my way, life has lost all
its flavour.

My children, what we're experiencing is not
Poseidon's rage.
But it *is* that of an unknown god who spreads
hatred and violence.
What did we do wrong, to deserve this?
We didn't besiege Troy, and we desecrated no
temples either.
Children, what's that you're crying out for?
Vengeance?

'Dear Father, if we call for vengeance then we're joining in with the ones who killed Mama. Let's pray for her and for all humanity. That's the best way to honour her.'

'How dare you speak on our behalf, big brother? You call on us to pray for her, without doing anything? You don't want to punish the people who killed Mama? That's just like you!'

'Little brother, excuses for violence have always been found everywhere, but now we must try to be wise.'

'To hell with your wisdom! I'm furious. Grant me the courage to fight against those monsters who try to force their god and their way of living down our throats! Let's put together an army to crush those hateful idiots. I'm going to pray for someone to come along and show us the path to glory. And when our enemies have been defeated once and for all, I'll make sure that peace and justice reign!'

'You talk about peace with a sword in your hand? You call for justice while you're shedding blood?

Is that what's become of us? I'm going to release four doves to fly to all four corners of the world, to spread love as the only answer to hatred. And you'll go with them, my youngest son, you'll protect them, my little falcon.'

The death penalty

Abolishing the death penalty without having
to fear that the social order will be harmed:
that comes down to honouring God's grandest
creation, the human being. The death penalty
is nothing but a crime committed with society's
permission and approval.

The heart

Bathing in love, floating on the river of life: nothing justifies hatred, nothing necessitates hate. Even the most terrible ordeals and the greatest disappointments won't make us bow to a jargon or an ideology that calls for hatred and destruction.

Let's move on, relying on our hearts and our reason, with conviction, whether that's religious or otherwise. Let's tap into love, that inexhaustible resource that comes from the heart and not from beneath our feet.

The wrongdoers

'If you think that taking innocent lives and
creating traumas is a form of justice, even of
God's justice, then you and I don't belong to
the same religion.'

That's what I'd say to them.

By showing acceptance, by listening to each other,
we could have talked about the injustice in the
world. There would be clear differences between
the way I look at Islam and their black-and-white
interpretation of it. The problem with such people
is that everything proceeds from the logic of
hatred, and I don't feel that hatred. They have
lost their humanity and dehumanise others.

You can't answer an injustice with another
injustice, that makes no sense. You may be

completely confused, totally desperate, but that can never justify hate or atrocities.

I don't understand how you can react to the injustice of global capitalism with this kind of Islamic obscurantism. A return to the 'harmonious' early days of Islam? Then you've forgotten that three of the first four caliphs were murdered. Creating a utopia from one day to the next? That's always gone hand-in-hand with destruction. Living the way they did in the Middle Ages? With WhatsApp?

Molenbeek

So you want to get out of Molenbeek? Fine,
but then don't go straight to Syria. Go to the
four corners of the earth, see how beautiful the
world is, discover other cultures. And if you go to
Damascus, the city Ibn Battuta called a paradise
on earth, then don't go there to destroy it,
but to admire it.

Of course, there are social problems in
Molenbeek. It's a community with a large
Moroccan population and unemployment here is
sky-high. But the Molenbeek I see and hear about
in the media is scarier than the community I know.
You'd almost think it was Kabul!

For me, Molenbeek is the community I grew
up in and where I have been happy. It's also the
community where, after Loubna's death,

I met with compassion from every generation, friendliness and a smile, from both the pious and the less pious, from the bearded ones and from the street corner boys. I've been helped by everyday citizens, by colleagues, Loubna's colleagues. True solidarity still exists in the Muslim community. Molenbeek is also the neighbourhood where the women's associations are very active. And where I still play football with my friends.

Morocco

A couple of days after the funeral service, they brought the coffin. Two thousand people met to pray in Brussels' Great Mosque. The next day we flew to Morocco. She was buried in Salé, where her father was from.

Prayers came in from all over the world, in the names of all the gods; it was magnificent, such powerful, positive energy. Nothing but love, nothing but strength, a religion, really. The religion of love.

The fact that I belong to two countries is a fortunate accident. I'm a child of Brussels, but I also feel supported by Morocco.

Along with the families of the other victims, we were received by King Filip of Belgium. It was a

lovely meeting; he showed a lot of empathy.
It was as though he had lost members of his
own family.

In July, I received a call from one of his councillors.
The king had invited us to come. That was a
huge honour. The hotel and the trip were paid for.
My three children, my mother-in-law and I spoke
in private with His Majesty at his palace. It was
simply incredible. As though we had ended up in
the thousand-and-one nights. The architecture,
the protocol…

The king made me feel at ease. My children were
making noise, but he said: 'I understand, I have
children of my own.' He was very personable.
He said that I was a good father and that he felt
responsibility towards my children. I don't know
what that means in practical terms but, coming
from the king, it sounded very powerful to a
father who is completely beside himself. I felt
like he helped me back on my feet.

What touched me most was that he said that
Loubna's death had moved him deeply, and that

he considered her a textbook example of successful integration. I'm still amazed to think that she had succeeded in making an impression on people in even the highest circles. To hear that my wife was an example of integration, that was a unique and powerful moment for me. I feel great affection for the king for having said that. He wouldn't have had to.

It seems to me that there is a clear difference between the Moroccan and the Saudi-Arabian versions of Islam. With us, the king is the guardian of centuries-old traditions. The Moroccan tradition is about tolerance. At a certain point, when we were there, I found myself sitting at the table with a Moroccan Jew. That was completely normal, he was a fully-fledged Moroccan.

Our identity as Moroccans, the king told me, has to do with being good citizens, wherever we live. That is what it means to be a Moroccan. Promoting a society in which we live together. Based on that thought, I want to dedicate myself to strengthening the friendship between the two peoples who are dearest to my heart.

Two countries

What I really like about Belgium is the concept of *belgitude*. That you don't take yourself too seriously. That appeals to me. When you're abroad, you hear people say that they like Belgians. That they are more lively and less chauvinistic than the French. In history, Belgium is spoken of as a mongrel country – without anything negative about that. We are a real crossroads and we feel very comfortable with that. I am fond of this part of the world, where I was born and which has given me the chance to be who I am today.

What I like about Morocco is the quality of life there. There is less frustration, less anger. The young people are much calmer and politer than the young Moroccans in Brussels. When a funeral procession comes along, everyone rises to their

feet respectfully. Death is not muffled away.
The relationship with death is different. When
the procession has passed, everyone realises what
a privilege it is to be alive, and how important it is
to go on smiling, despite everything.

Depths

Even the most devout of persons has doubts at times.
Your faith is something you have to nurture.
Sometimes you find yourself standing at the
edge of the abyss of doubt.

I have to admit that it's the king's words that
keep me going. Otherwise I don't know where
to turn. A thick fog. I have no prospects. I don't
go to work, I don't drive the metro, don't see my
colleagues. That all belongs to another time.
It reminds me of my life with Loubna.

It's so true, what Khalil Gibran wrote in his lovely
book *The Prophet*: 'Love knows not its own depth
until the hour of separation.'

To love – and to never forget to express that love
as often as you can to your beloved.

The children talk about their mother all the time. In their smiles, I still find strength and meaning. But the challenge is to tell them that the world is lovely, that people are good, despite what has happened to us. I have to remain stoical in order to keep going. If I collapse, it's done with.

Beauty

Life no longer tastes the same to me, but the setting sun is still glorious.

The essence

The story of Loubna and Mohamed is not the
essence. It's only a love story, like so many. What
it's primarily about is Loubna, who disappears
under unbelievable, unthinkable circumstances.
And about what she leaves behind. The fruits of
love – her children – and our everlasting love and
a powerful message.

Loubna is my Helen of Troy. She doesn't cause
a war, but spreads love, even after her death.
She is an eternal princess who goes on living in
this message of peace and love. It's not given to
everyone to die and then to have your death take
on meaning.

Belonging

Vertical love from the Almighty for those he has
created; horizontal love that we must spread over
all of humanity.

When I meet someone of another faith who allows
themselves to be led by love, I have the feeling
that we share the same religion. It's a little like
a poem I read long ago. By Imam Al-Ghazali,
I believe it was, the great mystic in the history of
Islam: 'Go to the far reaches of your religion, and
there you will find the religion of others.'

In this time of globalization, it's important to be
aware of your own culture and history, but also of
the culture and history of others. Behind everything
that divides us and separates us, all inhabitants of
this earth are bound together; black people, white
people, Jews, Buddhists, Muslims and atheists.

History shows us that it is possible to live together. Shortly after the Prophet died, the Muslims of Damascus had no place to pray, but they were allowed to pray in the church belonging to the Christians. During the Reformation, the Anabaptists, who the Church said were heretics, saw the Turks as their brothers. In the Vatican, Raphael painted a fresco of the great Averroës, a Muslim, in the very heart of Christianity.

It is a great thing to be part of a people, but above all we are a part of humanity. Every child must be taught first and foremost that he is a part of this world. That he can identify with all the great souls in history. That he may love Aristotle, Plato, Rumi, Sun Tzu, Confucius, Mother Teresa… That he may identify with each and every one of them. They belong to him as well. They belong to all of us.

Cosmopolitanism is a culture that nestles down beside the local culture, but doesn't replace it. I bring my culture along with me, but not so that I can put down the culture of another. I feel like saying: 'Tell me about yourself, you who come from so far away. Tell me the story of your people. I want to hear it, not in order to judge you, but because your story is my story too.'

You can lose your culture, your faith, your country, but you don't lose your humanity.

Education

Diversity should become the norm, starting from the youngest years, by stressing the importance of citizenship and of acknowledging differences. Assimilation, becoming fully absorbed by a new culture, makes no sense. Its opposite, locking yourself up within your own community, makes no sense either. A community is a gateway, not a fortress.

It's important that we teach young people to express their emotions. Art and poetry can play a role in that. With art and poetry, we could give young people a means to develop their artistic sensitivity, which is intrinsically connected to a love for beauty.

Let's encourage our young people to express their love for their parents, brothers, sisters and partners, but also for a stranger who happens by and is nothing but a brother in humanity.

Those who ban music, art and poetry deprive people of their hearing, their sight and the experience of the loveliest thing that can arise from inside of all of us.

Jihad

I vow to reply to this injustice, as an homage to who Loubna was and always will be, and as an act of respect, admiration and love towards all my human brothers and sisters, regardless of their religion, beliefs, ethnicity or sexual inclination.

In the ordeal I have to go through I feel more like a 'jihadist' than the greatest warrior. I am a jihadist for love. Don't ask me to hate, I would rather die!

In classical Arabic, the word jihad means 'struggle'. The jihad has been used to motivate troops, to wage war. That happened in the name of God, and in the eyes of a believer there can be no better reason than that. But originally, jihad means 'struggle'. That is the main definition: the struggle against yourself, against your passions, your urges.

A true jihadist is someone who does not explode in anger, no matter what the situation. He may feel rage, but it's so easy to hit someone or use violence. It is the stupidest reaction possible. Real jihadism is an effort made towards yourself, towards your thoughts. The jihadist thirsts after knowledge, does his best to meet others halfway, even when they are uncooperative. The jihadist doesn't lose courage, he keeps his smile and acknowledges the other person's humanity.

The Prophet often said: 'Do not become angry, then you will enter Paradise.'*
He even gave practical advice on how to calm down. 'If one of you is angry when he is standing, let him sit down so that the anger will leave him. Otherwise, let him lie down.'**

* Hadith, Saheeh al-Jaami, 7374
** Hadith, Saheeh al-Jaami, 694

This book

What is this book?
A poem.
An homage, an ode to Loubna.
A response to humanity, not to madness.
The expression of pain, but also of resilience –
through love.
Love, humanity, faith – I think that sums it up.

I hope that it benefits everyone who reads it.
My wish is to comfort all hearts.
If we find calmness, it will be easier for us
to progress.
Only a fool would choose not to live in peace.

Humanity

Seeing as I am first of all a human being and only secondly a Muslim, it's logical that I give pride of place to humanist values.

No matter whether I am a son of Adam or the product of evolution, my humanity implies three fundamental values: the inviolability of life, free will and brotherly ties with other people.

The inviolability of life means that you may never encroach on another person's life, just as I of course don't want someone to put an end to mine. Convictions and views may differ ever so widely, but this can never justify a murder. Every life is sacred.

Freedom of the will is the ability to choose your own path in life. You can choose to be a believer or not, whether you accept a given way of thinking or not. The free will gives the soul the freedom to blossom forth. That makes your thinking so much more interesting, so much deeper.

Brotherhood means that you say: 'My equal, my beloved brother in humanity, we probably don't agree on everything, but that doesn't matter. That won't keep us from sharing a meal together, in good cheer and mutual respect.'

Politics

I believe that these same principles should apply
in politics too. Always acknowledge that the
other is, first and foremost, a person. Always try
to summon up empathy for his views, without
passing judgement right away.

It's easy for me to put myself in the shoes of a
Palestinian or an Israeli. I can acknowledge the
injustice under which the Palestinians suffer.
Acknowledge that Gaza has become an open-air
prison. Acknowledge that the word 'colonists',
which seems to bother no one, reminds us of
dark periods in history.

But at the same time, I can put myself in the
position of an Israeli and acknowledge that
he is trying to find the best way to live with
his neighbours. To jointly acknowledge and

commemorate the Holocaust, so that it never happens again. But also, to understand that many young people have a hard time reconciling the focus on that historical suffering with the silence concerning their own, more recent suffering. Acknowledging that the ball is now in your court.

The discourse of hatred from Palestinian quarters only makes the Israeli extremists cling even more desperately to their policies. One side feeds upon the other, and nothing is solved. In the long run, the price is paid with the lives of the people themselves.

Each person killed is one too many, whether it's a Palestinian or an Israeli. An attack or bombing is never justifiable. That's my conviction as a pacifist. One needs to be indignant and loudly demand a dialogue, in order to find a liveable solution. There are people of good will on both sides. Jews and Palestinians are so much alike.

Honesty

Let's apply those same, fundamental values to the relations between the sexes.

Polygamy, according to the Koran, is tolerated, but tolerating something is not the same as encouraging it – on the contrary. In our day, Muslims in the West tend to marry for love, because of the dreams and goals they share. Still, after a few years some men start getting bored and decide to go looking further afield. They make use of an exception granted in the seventh century to soothe their conscience and justify their actions. But what has become of their standards? And what has become of their honesty? When they get married, they don't tell their wife that in twenty years' time they'll go looking for a new mate, do they? 'Piss off!' the girl would say. And rightly so.

You have to acknowledge the suffering of the wife who is suddenly exchanged for another. You can't dismiss her pain with an appeal to piety. You have to take her seriously, not say: 'Sure, I understand that it's difficult for you, a second wife, but accept it and you will go to Paradise.' That's complete rubbish. We need to show understanding when that woman decides to ask for a divorce. In my view, everything should be honest and above board from the very start.

The same goes for wearing a veil. It's not the man's place to force a woman to wear a veil. The woman is the one who wears it and has to live with it, so she should have her say in the matter too. Let's allow women to decide for themselves whether to defend the veil or not, and then, whatever their decision may be, let's continue to view them as fully-fledged Muslims.

Separation of religion and state

I'm a great advocate of the separation of church
and state. In my view, politics is the exact opposite
of religion. They have nothing to do with each
other. Religion is a largely vertical affair. Politics
is horizontal.

But when it comes to the new definition of
secularism, which says that all things religious
must be banned from public life, I'm much less
enthusiastic. I believe that people like Voltaire
would roll over in their graves if they heard what
some people, who call themselves 'humanists', are
saying about the separation of religion and state.
It has become a sort of fundamentalism that
excludes others – entire communities, in fact.
I'm against every form of fundamentalism,
including this one. It may be useful for winning
votes, but it's a disaster for individuals and society.

Prayer

The *Rubaiyat*, by the great poet Omar Khayyam,
contains the following quatrain:

> And if the Wine you drink, the Lip you press,
> End in the Nothing all Things end in – Yes –
> Then fancy while Thou art, Thou art but what
> Thou shalt be – Nothing – Thou shalt not be less.

I agree. Better lovers and drinkers than
hypocritical devotion. There are Muslims who
are only interested in outward appearance. When
it comes time to pray, they would stop even in
the middle of the motorway, so that everyone can
see how often and how well they pray. I think
you shouldn't burden other people with that.
You need to maintain a certain balance, a certain
perspective. Your religion should not be a banner.
Banner, by the way, is a military term.

For the moment at least, I no longer go to the
mosque, I avoid the crowd. I can't take that
any more. But praying remains a means for me
to communicate vertically. The fact that you put
aside your life five times a day and focus on high
is a sort of therapy. No matter how weighed down
you may be by the cares of the world, by emptying
yourself you rise above your doubts and your
anger and fix your eyes on the essence.

At night

My mind is racing, it's nighttime, it's cold.
Suddenly I am paralysed with fear.

Inside myself I see and hear a voice
that burns with a thousand whispering flames.
Is it because of the roaring silence
or the light of darkness?

'Peace be with you and with mankind.
Love your neighbour, even if he is bad.
Let everyone seek goodness in his convictions,
his faith, his philosophy.
All those who devote themselves to good
have a hero's bearing.
You make yourselves even lovelier
when you hold each other's hand.
I pray for today and for tomorrow.
Humanity, never forget that I am a part of you.

Later I'll return to the Almighty.
Never will you stand on the side of the unjust
and the evildoers.
You'll address yourself to good people from
all four corners of the earth.
Blessed be mankind.
May love triumph.'

Love

Love, that which drives me, lets me live
and live on.
Love, the foundation, the pedestal upon which
all faiths
must stand.
Love, the source from which all people
should be able to draw.
Love, the beginning of all blossoming.
Love, the refuge for those
choking on their tears.
Love, the embracing of an unknown soul.

Love cannot lead to hate, for joy
never leads to pain.
Love knows only mercy and forgiveness.
Love does not judge, love is innocent.
Love can be expressed and felt.
Love is nothing other than sharing and acceptance.

Love can be intimate, yet at the same time
everywhere.
If you are Love, then I share your religion.

The heart of every person is big enough
to include all of mankind.
All we have to do is open it, without fear.

From their earliest days, our young people must
grow up in love.
Without love, a child cannot blossom.
If a child cannot blossom, it can give no
love, later on.

A life without love is a world without the sun.
I need love like the air I breathe.
Like the water I drink.

Loubna,
Love of my life,
Till I draw my last breath,
You remain in my soul.

Final strophe

If I had not gone through what I went through
If no one had ever given me a turn to speak
If no one had given me the chance to speak out
loud.

You would never have heard what I have to say.

I, the metro driver,
was a Muslim like so many of the others
you never hear
you never see

But of whom there are oh-so many.

Afterword

A Jihad for Love consists of texts written by Mohamed El Bachiri after the attacks of 22 March, 2016 and remarks of his noted by David Van Reybrouck during an extensive interview on 2 and 3 February, 2017 in the Brussels communities of Anderlecht and Molenbeek. David Van Reybrouck also saw to the organization of the texts.

The original French version was translated into Dutch by Manik Sarkar and reworked by David Van Reybrouck.

The authors would like to thank Jeanne Lefèvre for her practical assistance, and Fatima Zibouh for her support during the writing. Mohamed would sincerely like to thank his mother, his father, his brothers and sisters for all their support in his loss, and to honour his mother-in-law, Loubna's mother, for her strength, faith and courage.